THE BOOK OF CATHOLIC PRAYERS

Daily Devotions for Peace and Purpose

By E. Paige

2

Copyright 2016 The Vintage Archives

http://www.The-Vintage-Archives.com

All Rights Reserved. No part of this book may be reproduced in any form or by any means without prior written consent of the publisher, except brief quotes used in reviews.

TABLE OF CONTENTS

Introduction ... 5

The Lords Prayer ... 6

The Hail Mary ... 8

The Glory Be Prayer ... 9

Spiritual Communion ... 10

An Act of Faith ... 12

An Act of Love ... 13

An Act of Contrition ... 14

Anima Christi ... 15

Evening Prayers ... 16

Guardian Angel Prayer ... 17

Meal Time Prayers ... 18

Memorare ... 19

Morning Prayers ... 20

Prayers to The Holy Spirit ... 21

The Three O' Clock Prayer ... 22

The Golden Arrow ... 23

The Apostles' Creed ... 24

The Divine Mercy Chaplet ... 26

How to Pray the Rosary ... 29

Introduction

BY incorporating daily prayer into your life you are opening yourself up to a wonderful world of possibilities. Not only can daily prayer change your life by developing a richer relationship with God you will also find peace and purpose in your life, something we can all use in these chaotic times. Prayer not only establishes a relationship with God but it also helps in maintaining that relationship with Him. Jesus constantly went before God in prayer to determine God's will and direction. Jesus is a perfect example of a life lived by prayer that offers purpose, answers, and most importantly, a relationship with God the Father.

Why Pray? "The earnest prayer of a righteous person has great power and wonderful results." James5:16

There are hundreds, if not thousands of great Catholic prayers available to you but what I wanted to focus on in this book are the prayers that will help you find peace, purpose and to connect with God on a daily basis.

The Lords Prayer

The Lord's Prayer, also known as Our Father, is a prayer that was composed by our Lord Jesus Christ Himself and is a central prayer in Christianity. This prayer reflects the wishes of its Divine Author.

There are two versions of The Lords Prayer. The first version presented in the Book of Matthew and the second version coming from the Book of Luke.

From the Book of Matthew 6:9-13

Our Father,
who art in heaven,
hallowed be thy name;
thy kingdom come;
thy will be done on earth as it is in heaven.
Give us this day our daily bread;
and forgive us our trespasses
as we forgive those who trespass against us;
and lead us not into temptation,
but deliver us from evil.
Amen.

From the Book of Luke 11:2-4

"Father,

hallowed be your name.

Your kingdom come.

Give us each day our daily bread,

and forgive us our sins,

for we ourselves forgive everyone who is indebted to us.

And lead us not into temptation."

The Hail Mary

The Hail Mary has inspired much devotion to Jesus and His Blessed Mother. This beautiful prayer has given people the graces, strength, and spiritual protection they've needed for hundreds of thousands of years.

Hail Mary, full of grace,
The Lord is with Thee;
Blessed art thou among women,
And blessed is the fruit of thy womb, Jesus.
Holy Mary, Mother of God,
Pray for us sinners,
Now and at the hour of our death.
Amen.

The Glory Be Prayer

The Glory Be prayer reaffirms the eternal glory of our "God in Three Persons, Blessed Trinity. The prayer dates back many centuries and is known also by its Latin name and version as the *Gloria Patri.* Many people make the sign of the cross when reciting this prayer.

Glory be to the Father,
And to the Son,
And to the Holy Spirit.
As it was in the beginning, is now,
And ever shall be,
World without end.
Amen.

Spiritual Communion

The best way to receive Christ is in Holy Communion at Mass but sometimes life gets in the way, preventing us from attending Mass as often as we would like but you can still reach out to Him by making a Spiritual Communion in prayer! St. Thomas Aquinas defined a Spiritual Communion as "an ardent desire to receive Jesus in the Most Holy Sacrament and in lovingly embracing Him as if we had actually received Him." You can make a Spiritual Communion as often as you'd like and wherever you'd like.

My Jesus, I believe that you are present in the most Blessed Sacrament.
I love You above all things and I desire to receive You into my soul.
Since I cannot now receive You sacramentally, come at least spiritually into my heart.
I embrace You as if You have already come, and unite myself wholly to You.
Never permit me to be separated from You.
Amen.

An Act of Faith

One of the best gifts God gave us is faith. With the power of faith, God has given us a true grace to completely trust Him and His word. The Act of Faith prayer does a wonderful job of capturing the full essence of our trust in Him.

O my God, I firmly believe that you are one God in three Divine Persons, Father, Son, and Holy Spirit; I believe that your Divine Son became man, and died for our sins, and that He will come to judge the living and the dead. I believe these and all the truths the Holy Catholic Church teaches because You have revealed them, who can neither deceive nor be deceived.

An Act of Hope

With God we are reminded that there is no place for despair regardless of what life throws in our path. There is always a light at the end of the tunnel, even when the tunnel seems endless. The Act of Hope prayer reminds us of this.

O my God, relying on Your almighty power and infinite mercy and promises, I hope to obtain pardon of my sins, the help of Your grace, and life everlasting, through the merits of Jesus Christ, my Lord and Redeemer.

An Act of Love

Love is one of God's greatest gifts to us. Love is one of three theological virtues, along with faith and hope. Jesus made it very clear in the Gospels that we show our love for Him in how we treat other people, and that He will forgive us as much as we forgive them.

O my God, I love you above all things, with my whole heart and soul, because you are all-good and worthy of all love. I love my neighbor as myself for the love of you. I forgive all who have injured me, and I ask pardon of all whom I have injured.

An Act of Contrition

The Act of Contrition is a prayer in which we ask God to forgive our sins. There are two types of contrition: perfect and imperfect. Both types of contrition are reflected in this version of the prayer.

O my God, I am heartily sorry for having offended Thee, and I detest all my sins, because I dread the loss of Heaven and the pains of Hell, but most of all because they offend Thee, my God, Who art all-good and deserving of all my love. I firmly resolve, with the help of Thy grace to confess my sins, to do penance and to amend my life. Amen.

Anima Christi

The Anima Christi, also known as Soul of Christ, is a prayer allowing us the opportunity to ask our Lord for comfort, strength, and guidance. It provides us a chance to meditate on His Passion and pray for His help to gain Eternal Life.

Soul of Christ, sanctify me.
Body of Christ, save me.
Blood of Christ, inebriate me.
Water from the side of Christ, wash me.

Passion of Christ, strengthen me.
O Good Jesus, hear me.
Within Thy wounds hide me.
Suffer me not to be separated from thee.
From the malignant enemy defend me.
In the hour of my death call me.
And bid me come unto Thee,
That with all Thy saints,
I may praise thee
Forever and ever.
Amen.

Evening Prayers

Taking time at the end of your day to thank God for your daily blessings and asking Him for forgiveness is a wonderful time to take stock of your daily transgressions. Evening prayers also present a wonderful opportunity for you to take an honest look at your life with our Lord.

I adore You, my God, and I love You with all my heart. I thank you for having created me, for having made me a Christian, and for having preserved me this day. Pardon me for the evil I have done today. If I have done anything good, be pleased to accept it. Protect me while I take my rest and deliver me from all dangers. May your grace be always with me. Amen.

Oh Lord, we pray you to visit this home and drive from it all snares of the enemy. Let Your holy angels dwell in it to preserve us in peace; and let Your blessing be always upon us. Through Christ our Lord. Amen.

Protect us, Lord, as we stay awake; watch over us as we sleep, that awake, we may keep watch with Christ, and asleep, rest in his peace.

Guardian Angel Prayer

Believe it or not but everyone has a special Guardian Angel watching over them. The Guardian Angel prayer allows you the chance to pay special tribute to this divine being.

Angel of God, my guardian dear, to whom God's love commits me here, ever this day [or night] be at my side, to light and guard, to rule and guide. Amen.

Meal Time Prayers

Meal time prayers allow us the opportunity to stay close to God as we ask for His blessings as He gives us "our daily Bread". There are two prayers that you can recite during your meals. One is before you break bread and the other is after your meal is complete.

GRACE BEFORE MEALS
Bless us, O Lord and these Your gifts which we are about to receive from Your bounty. Through Christ our Lord. Amen.

GRACE AFTER MEALS
We give you thanks, Almighty God, for all Your benefits, who live and reign, world without end. Amen. May the souls of the faithful departed, through the mercy of God, rest in peace. Amen.

Memorare

Memorare is a prayer which reminds us that we have an advocate and protector in the mother of our Lord, the Blessed Virgin Mary. Memorare invites us to ask the Blessed Mother for her assistance and her grace when we have difficulties approaching God in our prayers.

REMEMBER, O most gracious Virgin Mary, that never was it known that anyone who fled to thy protection, implored thy help, or sought thy intercession was left unaided. Inspired with this confidence, I fly to thee, O Virgin of virgins, my Mother; to thee do I come; before thee I stand, sinful and sorrowful. O Mother of the Word Incarnate, despise not my petitions, but in thy mercy hear and answer me. Amen.

Morning Prayers

Morning prayers are an excellent way to refresh your soul. Morning prayers should be treated as a way to get closer to God. By giving God your day in prayer first thing in the morning, you get "the clear air of heaven," flowing into your heart.

O Jesus, through the Immaculate Heart of Mary, I offer You my prayers, works, joys and sufferings of this day for all the intentions of Your Sacred Heart, in union with the Holy Sacrifice of the Mass throughout the world, in reparation for my sins, for the intentions of all my relatives and friends, and in particular for the intentions of the Holy Father. Amen.

Prayers to The Holy Spirit

Prayers to The Holy Spirit also referred to as Pentecost Prayers are prayers that can be said ayear round and is a great way to ask for God's assistance when we are facing problems, or simply need help bearing our crosses.

We beseech you, O Lord, let the power of the Holy Spirit be always with us; let it mercifully purify our hearts, and safeguard us from all harm. Grant this through Christ our Lord, Amen.

May the Comforter, Who proceeds from You, enlighten our minds, we beseech you, O Lord, and guide us, as Your Son has promised, into all truth. We ask this through Christ, our Lord, Amen.

Holy Spirit, Sweet guest of My Soul, Abide In Me and Grant That I May Ever abide in Thee.

The Three O' Clock Prayer

When your feeling down or like no one cares the Three O' Clock Prayer is exactly what you need. This prayer helps remind us that we always have someone there, Jesus Christ.

Dear Lord, remembering the hour when You experienced death
So that we might have Eternal Life,
May we appreciate in our hearts the necessity of Your sacrifice for us
And with Your help, Your guidance, and Your grace,
May we be made worthy of it.

The Golden Arrow

The Golden Arrow is a vary important prayer that Jesus gave to Sister Mary of St. Peter in August of 1843. The Golden Arrow is intended as an act of reparation for the profanation of Sunday and of Holy Days of Obligation as well.

May the most holy, most sacred, most adorable,
most incomprehensible and unutterable Name of God
be always praised, blessed, loved, adored
and glorified in Heaven, on earth,
and under the earth,
by all the creatures of God,
and by the Sacred Heart of Our Lord Jesus Christ,
in the Most Holy Sacrament of the Altar.
Amen.

The Apostles' Creed

The Apostles' Creed is a very important prayer can be traced all the way back to the 7th or 8th century AD. This prayer reflects the Apostles' teachings, as well as those found in the New Testament.

I believe in God, the Father Almighty,
Creator of heaven and earth; (The 1st article)
And in Jesus Christ, His only Son, our Lord; (The 2nd)

Who was conceived by the Holy Spirit,
Born of the Virgin Mary, (The 3rd)
Suffered under Pontius Pilate,
Was crucified, died, and was buried. (The 4th)
He descended into hell;
The third day he rose again from the dead; (The 5th)
He ascended into Heaven,
And is seated at the right hand of God, the Father Almighty;
(The 6th)
From thence he shall come to judge the living and the dead.
(The 7th)
I believe in the Holy Spirit, (The 8th)
The Holy Catholic Church,
The Communion of Saints, (The 9th)

The forgiveness of sins, (The 10th)

The resurrection of the body, (The 11th)

And life everlasting. Amen. (The 12th)

The Divine Mercy Chaplet

The Divine Mercy Chaplet is a prayer created by our Lord to help foster devotion to His Divine Mercy. The prayer was taught to Saint Maria Faustina Kowalska in 1953 during one of His revelations to her.

Before beginning this prayer make the sign of the cross. Then you can pray either, or both, of these two opening prayers:

You expired, Jesus, but the source of life gushed forth for souls, and the ocean of mercy opened up for the whole world. O Fount of Life, unfathomable Divine Mercy, envelop the whole world and empty Yourself out upon us.

Or:

O Blood and Water, which gushed forth from the Heart of Jesus as a fountain of Mercy for us, I trust in You!

On the first three beads, say the Our Father prayer.

Our Father, Who art in heaven, hallowed be Thy name; Thy kingdom come; Thy will be done on earth as it is in heaven. Give us this day our daily bread; and forgive us our trespasses as we forgive those who trespass against us; and lead us not into temptation, but deliver us from evil, Amen.

Then the Hail Mary prayer.

Hail Mary, full of grace. The Lord is with thee. Blessed art thou amongst women, and blessed is the fruit of thy womb, Jesus. Holy Mary, Mother of God, pray for us sinners, now and at the hour of our death, Amen.

Next is the Apostles Creed.

I believe in God, the Father Almighty, Creator of heaven and earth; and in Jesus Christ, His only Son, our Lord, Who was conceived by the Holy Spirit, born of the Virgin Mary, suffered under Pontius Pilate, was crucified, died, and was buried. He descended into hell; the third day he rose again from the dead; He ascended into Heaven, and is seated at the right hand of God, the Father Almighty; from thence he shall come to judge the living and the dead; I believe in the Holy Spirit, the Holy Catholic Church, the Communion of Saints, the forgiveness of sins, the resurrection of the body, and the life everlasting. Amen.

You now pray the rest of the Divine Mercy Chaplet in the following manner, for each of the five decades on the large bead say:

Eternal Father, I offer you the Body and Blood, Soul and Divinity of Your Dearly Beloved Son, Our Lord, Jesus Christ, in atonement for our sins and those of the whole world.

On the ten small beads for each of the five decades, recite.

For the sake of His sorrowful Passion, have mercy on us and on the whole world.

After having completed the prayer's five decades, you recite the following, three times.

Holy God, Holy Mighty One, Holy Immortal One, have mercy on us and on the whole world.

You can conclude the Divine Mercy Chaplet with the following closing prayer, which is optional.

Eternal God, in whom mercy is endless and the treasury of compassion inexhaustible, look kindly upon us and increase Your mercy in us, that in difficult moments we might not despair nor become despondent, but with great confidence submit ourselves to Your holy will, which is Love and Mercy itself.

How to Pray the Rosary

The purpose of the Rosary is to help keep in memory certain principal events or mysteries in the history of our salvation, and to thank and praise God for them. Learning how to say The Rosary can seem like a daunting task, until you actually learn how to do so. However, it is a task that is well worth it. When saying The Rosary we are educating ourselves on what the mysteries contain and what those mysteries promise. The mysteries refer to a particular event in the lives of Mary and Jesus. When you learn how to say The Rosary you are truly bonding with Our Lord and His Blessed Mother. Can you imagine a better feeling than that?

Getting started is very simple as all you will need is a pair of Rosary beads.

1. Make the sign of the Cross and say the Apostles' Creed prayer.

I believe in God, the Father Almighty,

Creator of heaven and earth; (The 1st article)

And in Jesus Christ, His only Son, our Lord; (The 2nd)

Who was conceived by the Holy Spirit,

Born of the Virgin Mary, (The 3rd)

Suffered under Pontius Pilate,

Was crucified, died, and was buried. (The 4th)

He descended into hell;

The third day he rose again from the dead; (The 5th)

He ascended into Heaven,

And is seated at the right hand of God, the Father Almighty;

(The 6th)

From thence he shall come to judge the living and the dead.

(The 7th)

I believe in the Holy Spirit, (The 8th)

The Holy Catholic Church,

The Communion of Saints, (The 9th)

The forgiveness of sins, (The 10th)

The resurrection of the body, (The 11th)

And life everlasting. Amen. (The 12th)

2. Recite the Our Father Prayer.

Our Father, Who art in heaven

Hallowed be Thy Name;

Thy kingdom come,

Thy will be done,

on earth as it is in heaven.

Give us this day our daily bread,

and forgive us our trespasses,

as we forgive those who trespass against us;

and lead us not into temptation,

but deliver us from evil. Amen.

3. Say three Hail Marys.

Hail Mary, full of grace.

Our Lord is with thee.

Blessed art thou among women,

and blessed is the fruit of thy womb,

Jesus.

Holy Mary, Mother of God,

pray for us sinners,

now and at the hour of our death.

Amen.

4. Say the Glory Be To The Father prayer.

Glory be to the Father, and to the Son, and to the Holy Spirit.

As it was in the beginning, is now, and ever shall be, world without end.

Amen.

5. Announce the First Mystery and then say.

Our Father, Who art in heaven

Hallowed be Thy Name;

Thy kingdom come,

Thy will be done,

on earth as it is in heaven.

Give us this day our daily bread,

and forgive us our trespasses,

as we forgive those who trespass against us;

and lead us not into temptation,

but deliver us from evil. Amen.

6. Say Ten Hail Marys while meditating on the mystery.

Hail Mary, full of grace.

Our Lord is with thee.

Blessed art thou among women,

and blessed is the fruit of thy womb,

Jesus.

Holy Mary, Mother of God,

pray for us sinners,

now and at the hour of our death.

7. Say the Glory to be The Father.

Glory be to the Father and to the Son and to the Holy Spirit.

As it was in the beginning is now, and ever shall be, world without end.

Amen.

8. Announce the Second Mystery and then say the Our Father prayer.

Our Father, Who art in heaven

Hallowed be Thy Name;

Thy kingdom come,

Thy will be done,

on earth as it is in heaven.

Give us this day our daily bread,

and forgive us our trespasses,

as we forgive those who trespass against us;

and lead us not into temptation,

but deliver us from evil. Amen.

9. Repeat steps 6 and 7 and continue with the Third, Fourth and Fifth Mysteries in the same manner.

10. After the Rosary recite the Hail Holy Queen prayer:

HAIL, HOLY QUEEN, Mother of Mercy, our life, our sweetness and our hope! To thee do we cry, poor banished children of Eve; to thee do we send up our sighs, mourning and weeping in this valley of tears. Turn then, most gracious advocate, thine eyes of mercy toward us, and after this our exile, show unto us the blessed fruit of thy womb, Jesus. O clement, O loving, O sweet Virgin Mary!

11. After reciting the Hail Holy Queen prayer, recite the following.

LET US PRAY: O God, whose only begotten Son, by his life, death and resurrection, has purchased for us the rewards of eternal life, grant, we beseech thee, that meditating upon these mysteries of the most holy Rosary of the Blessed Virgin Mary, we may imitate what they contain and obtain what they promise, through the same Christ our Lord. Amen.

Copyright 2016 The Vintage Archives

http://www.The-Vintage-Archives.com

All Rights Reserved. No part of this book may be reproduced in any form or by any means without prior written consent of the publisher, except brief quotes used in reviews.

Partners

Vintage Image Shoppe – High Quality Digital Image Downloads

https://www.etsy.com/shop/VintageImageShoppe

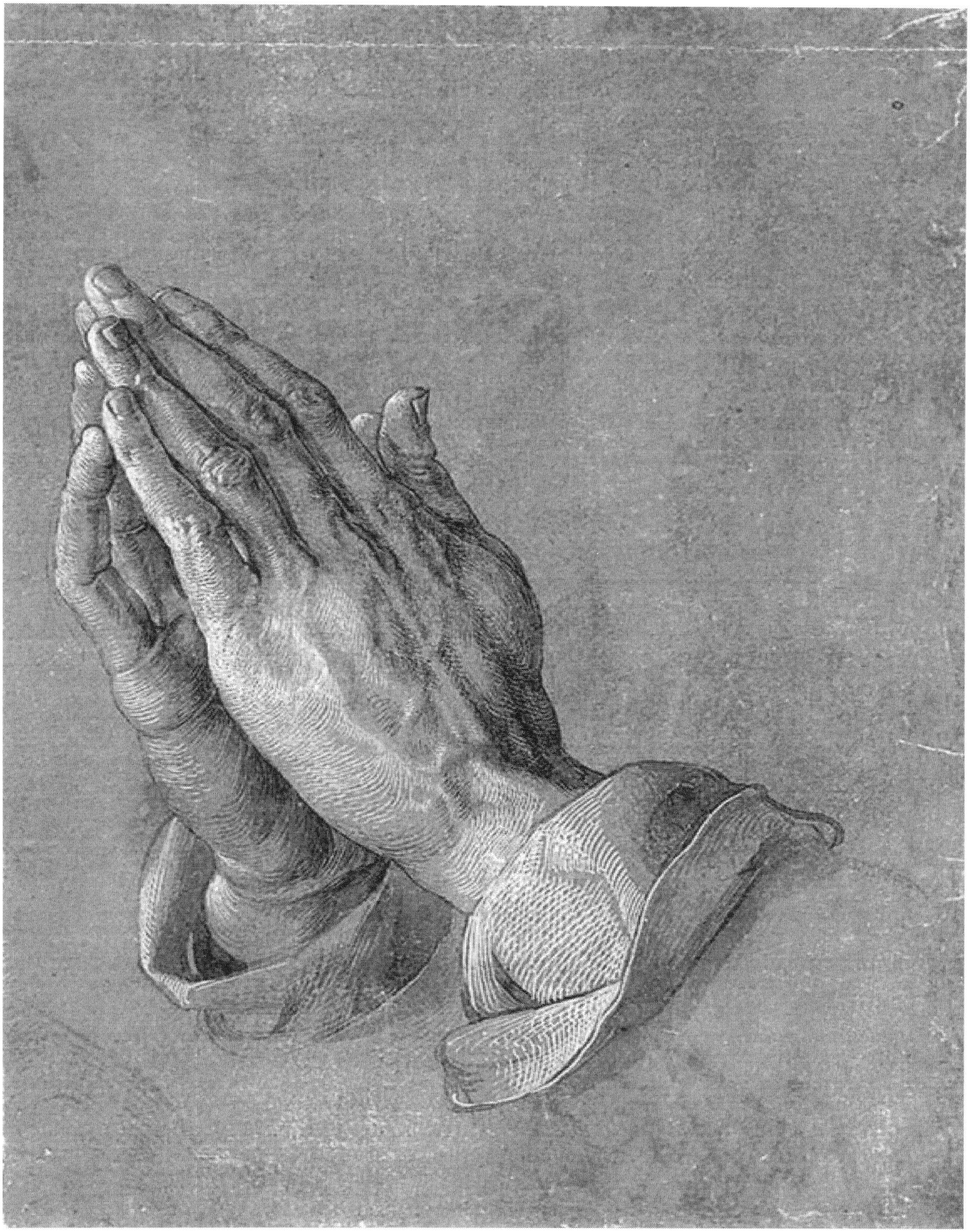

Printed in Great Britain
by Amazon